THE PROMISE:

I0408221

EMPOWERING

The Children Of America

&

Generations To Come!

by

Dennis Andrew Ball,

author, THE BALL DOCTRINE:

"Creating Peace & Prosperity In Every Nation!"

- 1 -

ISBN 13: 978-1543196870
10: 154319687X

DEDICATION

"THIS BOOK IS DEDICATED TO ALL THOSE

WHO FOUGHT & DIED FOR OUR LIBERTY

AND FREEDOM TO CREATE THE SOCIAL

CONTRACT THAT WAS FORMED AT THE

BATTLE OF YORKTOWN, VIRGINIA

OCTOBER 19, 1781

FOR THE BIRTH OF FREEDOM

FOR

OUR CHILDREN AND

GENERATIONS TO COME!"

TABLE OF CONTENTS

Dedication

Acknowledgment

Authors' Forward

————

ACKNOWLEDGMENT

*For The Countless Support Of The Publisher's
Staff That Made This Work Possible!*

Author's Forward

*The history of the United States would not be
complete if it were not for those gallant men and
women who in the face of tyranny, proceeded to do
something Special about it! This then is the
premise for* **The Promise: Empowering
The Children Of America &
Generations To Come!;** *to do something
positive to insure the way for countless generations
to come and advance that which was given to all of
us by those who gave and have given their all so
that their families and their children might have a
better life than they did. It is in this tradition
that the Promise of America and the Nation was*

5

born and is given to all of us freely as trustees to secure the blessings of Liberty to protect our Freedoms & Rights; those Freedoms and Rights All Of Us Have Been Endowed With By The Creator And To Cause Accountability by Those in Power to Act In Our BEST INTERESTS as the Government Of The People, By The People & For The People, Now and Forever, Amen!

6

1. *THE PROMISE!*

"Harry, will you give this to my children, thank you."

"DEAR CHARLOTTE – The War has turned and General Cornwallis took flight with his Army moved North. We continued to engage the British with the months that followed.

Cornwallis entrenched himself at Yorktown, Virginia. George Washington escaped from the North undetected to surround Cornwallis who could not retreat to the seas. It was blocked off by our long lost friends who had finally arrived, *the French.*

Though he eventually surrendered, Cornwallis hid in shame appointing his subordinate relinquishing his sword. With the War ending & our militia disbanding I take measure of what we have lost & what we have won.

My Hope & Prayer is that the sacrifice born by so many will spawn and fulfill ***the promise*** of our new nation. Tell the children and especially Susan that I will keep my promise as I will be returning to you all, soon." – Benjamin Martin, The Patriot, Sony Pictures, 2000.

"Tell the children and especially Susan that I will keep my Promise as I will be returning to you all, soon." - Benjamin

Ladies and Gentlemen; children, what was *fought and died fore,* for you and for me and a host of generations to Come was so Special that it dwarfs anything else ever accomplished by men in recorded human history.   The promise so articulated by Benjamin Martin is the premise for the forming of our government of, by and for the people. We the People, the

8

Government Power to the people to hold accountable those who would turn and abuse We The People.

Let it be said, that America's finest hours are yet to come because the Children Of America can make a contribution to not only our Nation but also the World!

We are the product of generations past, present and future with the belief that our rights come from God; NOT THE STATE at a great cost to those who fought and died for them! That was the Social Contract created in 1781 at Yorktown-Gloucester Bay, Virginia.

The monuments laid at the reefs of those so honored are a testament to the sacrifice of so many for the hope that their sacrifice would prevail. A proud nation was born and with it the greatest nation on earth in the history of man, "*AMERICA!*"

I ask for your support in this effort to show the miracle of an eight year war terminating in victory over the most powerful army on earth, the British Crown. Washington was a splendid choice by the Patriots to marshal all the assets to compensate and provide the support of defeating General Cornwallis and the British Empire. Let us proceed into the future making God's Covenant with America truly one of our own for our children and their futures! It is time to change the course of history to make our culture and society compatible once again with our ideals, beliefs and sacrifice to once again make our culture strong, durable and resilient for that which the greatest generation gave all for the procurement and blessings of liberty by their sacrifices. Can we do any less? This is "The Promise" given to all God's children to exercise and protect by preserving

10

and defending IT! - OUR CONSTITUTION OF THE UNITED STATES! ONE NATION UNDER GOD, INDIVISIBLE WITH LIBERTY & JUSTICE FOR ALL!

2. THE START!

Now, I want to tell you a story about what happened after the battle ended. The history of America is full of stories of people who began the process of settling the land for their families and loved ones. This was an extension of that which started prior to the Revolution of 1776. The Social Contract between the people and their government was the basis for this nation to grow and expand into a great society in spite of the War and issues of slavery, cheap labor and the Indian Nation.

It was a time when the young nation was now more than just 13 Colonies but a nation with a Congress, President and Judiciary. These three divisions of government as today, provided the basis for America to grow and expand both legally and morally. The Bible was the main book for reading and lots of

12

lessons from it where read to the children by adults in their family. The Bible became the foundation by which moral conduct was taught and measured and provided the support for families to raise their children accordingly.

Family was affirmed important for sustainability of society. The culture affirmed that families were important and that one could know something about their community by the reputation created by them.

Now that has <u>all</u> changed because of the negligence of this and previous generations.

I would hope that all of us get on the same page to do that which must get done.

The Social Contract that Lincoln spoke at Gettysburg was a reflection of its Origins at Yorktown, Virginia created October 19, 1781.

13

The Covenant established that power of government is Vested in The People. The Covenant God made with His People extended to the United States because many of the Founders who had God in their heart and the Rule Of Law on their lips requires us to also stand up and make our voices heard!

As Lincoln said "It is for us *'The Living'* to *finish the work that so many gave their lives on the battlefield.* I ask all of us, "Can We Do Any Less?".

What Lincoln witnessed was the carnage of humanity that so brutally portrayed itself before the nation and world. That on July 1, 1863 the beginning of the end of the American Civil War commenced at Gettysburg, Pennsylvania with the Address to the nation on the nineteenth of November, 1863.

14

Some *eighty-eight years prior to the carnage* That befell *the soldiers on both sides at Yorktown, Virginia is a reminder to us all how fragile freedom is and the price that is paid by our children to keep it.*

3. THE RACE!

Originally, the nation was engulfed with its own survival amongst themselves. From receiving mail to trading every week at the market place for their needs with the race for survival converted to a race for Independence!

Now, be not ignorant that there were also those of privilege that made themselves known but they too were not accepted by the English Ruling Class and would never be accepted by the snobbery of the English Monarchy; particularly the King and his Court, George The Third.

And while America was dealing with itself within their own communities, attitudes detrimental to the well being of the colonies were brewing amongst them all. No Political Correctness here, just raw emotion based on

16

fact and truth that impacted them all personally, including those that were as *slaves*.

"Lord, make me fast and accurate!", said Benjamin Martin(1).

These are the words of a farmer turned soldier that knew freedom is not free and that it comes to those who don't think like a *slave*. Though, General Washington was the nation's leader, he was also a farmer. His father died when he was just 10 working on the farm learning the ways of the weather and the land; would later work to his benefit. God was a part of these men's lives.

(1)"The Patriot", Sony Pictures.

The founders believed that as free people must act according to the dictates of "honor". The British also believed in "honor" as long as it served their purposes and their empire, the English Crown.

But because the ruling classes of England displayed and presented an arrogance of attitudes toward American Colonial culture, the Revolution of 1776 started with the upper classes within Colonial America because they believed that British Aristocracy would never accept them as equals, and so the conflict reigned permeating into every stratum of the two cultures.

So *is "The Promise", a portrait into the forces that created the most powerful tilt in World History empowering The Patriots to run the race to freedom and opportunity until being denied, they rebelled.*

Now, we must ask "Why has it taken this long for this nation to come to grips with the reality that America and the World are only as good as those who lead it?" Philosopher Kings

18

have pondered such questions that placed responsibility for the moral conduct and personal worth of a nation on the platform of history for all the world to see and judge.

Are we unaccountable for the actions of others Social Conduct than those who don't? That take an Oath to God & Country to uphold the value of *Life, Liberty and Pursuit of Happiness* would use, abuse and misuse us at our own expense? Are we not accountable that those who commit treason in our midst have not a higher standard to Answer?

It is in this context that we find ourselves today, entrenched in the battle of good versus evil, government venting itself in the diatribe of discourse that impacts everyone and places an undo burden upon each of us and our children that is unsustainable and will lead to only more of the same.

19

A web of lies and manipulations by those who take advantage of us yet justify themselves in their carefully crafted propaganda to deflect liability and accountability away from themselves by blaming others for their misdeeds. This is and was the core cause for anger that formed American Society by its people running the race to defeat the forces of evil controlling and manipulating themselves then and has come to revisit us now! What are WE going to do about it? That is a question all of us must answer leading all of us to ask:

"If We Are Not Working In The BEST INTERESTS of our family, Then Who's Interests Are we Working fore?"

<u>NOTES</u>

<u>QUESTIONNAIRE</u>

1. WHAT WAS THE DATE THE WAR WAS WON?

2. WHO LED THE CONTINENTAL ARMY TO VICTORY?

3. WHERE WAS THE FINAL BATTLE FOUGHT?

4. WHO JOINED WASHINGTON AT YORKTOWN?

5. WHO IS BENJAMIN MARTIN COMPARED?

6. WHO SIGNED THE TREATY OF VERSAILLES?

7. HOW MANY COLONIES BECAME STATES?

8. WHICH COLONY BECAME THE 1ST STATE?

9. WHO WAS THE DEFEATED COMMANDING BRITISH GENERAL?

10. WHO UTTERED "GIVE ME LIBERTY OR GIVE ME DEATH?"

answers: 1). October 19, 1781,   2). George Washington, 3).Gloucester Bay, Virginia, 4). The French Navy, 5).General Francis Marion, 6). Benjamin Franklin, John Jay, 7). 13 Colonies, 8). Delaware, 9). General Charles Cornwallis (British), 10). Patrick Henry.

FREE SPACE

4. THE GOAL!

"Out of the mouths of Babes Cometh the Course of History!" -   author unknown

From the Race to now the Goal, the history of America is littered with events that marked a turn in *her history.*

The Founder's did not know what to expect of others besides a strong *nationalism* that came from their commitment to their families and loved ones.

This permeated American Culture in the decades of the 18th & 19th centuries making way for the economic development of a strong middle class.

How this was implemented by the Ruling Classes during Colonial American Society was a product of rural agrarian productivity supporting society by the adage "If a man doesn't support his family, then he don't eat."

25

How different America has changed from a nation of Independence *to a Nation of entitlement* but unlike our predecessors, America has been dumbed down to allow a Ruling Elite to emerge and hold the nation hostage to a powerful Plutocracy that Abraham Lincoln was concerned would destroy the Republic. We are now living his concerns. We are also forced to take action to preserve and protect our nation and way of life from "isms" foreign to America but would want to take over our lands and Resources.

With the emergence of Violent Jihad, the World must strongly respond to the threats it poses.

The Social Contract demands America protects her borders and those who would be defiled by the lawless behavior imported to her. That is the job of every law enforcement officer and every citizen to Preserve our laws and our Constitution for the benefit and protection of our children and families.

This must be the Goal of America to preserve, protect and defend from threats both foreign and domestic for the benefit of our children & families.

"Think 1ˢᵗ What Our Country Has Become, Act & Do What Must Be Done!"

5. THE TEST!

Throughout the *early* history of America, the nation continued to challenge its citizens and the World to cause great problems since the final victory that was World War II . Now, the nation is faced with a number of both national and existential threats that have the potential of rewriting history and sacrificing the lives of those who gave their full measure and devotion so that many could live both now and in the future in relative peace, harmony and security.

However, that is being threatened by forces unfriendly to "Freedom" that would choose to enslave us or worse kill us! This then is the TEST!

What kind of nation are we to *remain*?

28

Shall we become docile and allow ourselves to be Swept about like a torrent on an angry sea? Or Shall we be motivated to DO that which is required to preserve, protect and defend ourselves and Our Freedoms from Exploitation by the State and Their abuse that is so near?

Within all of my writings, I attempt to shed my Wisdom and Knowledge to motivate all of us to *Action!*

The Social Contract born October 19, 1781

Gloucester Bay, Virginia still lives today though Greatly diminished from the dumbing down of Society by those in positions of leadership, authority and tutelage.

This can be reversed by the actions of

29

others who Know society has many moving parts like a fine watch all in *sync* with each other to tell time and keep things moving!

6. THE TIME!

I am reminded that history *can* and *does* repeat itself by the actions of others who use, abuse and misuse us for personal gain and profit.

Succinctly, this is the history of mankind. The question to be posed is how to Stop the abuse to others to assist us to live?

The sacrifices born by so few for so many is the bases for *The Promise!* With roots so firmly planted in the past do we dare reach out to the future? Are we a nation of leaders? Can we stand up to the test of time?

Nothing is guaranteed in life except the test of time. Let us embrace our future with vigor and certainty that our children and their children's children will have a chance to

31

survive and thrive.

This is then The Promise we all *Should* embrace!

Reflections of the past showed us what courage and valor can and will produce. Thank our soldiers for their service to preserve and protect our freedoms and rights fought and died by countless individuals who gave it all.

So many stories so little time we all are so grateful.

We all are accountable. We all are subjects of it.

I reflect what Generals Gates' & Marion contributed to the War For Independence and how during a time of indifference and stalemate, what others did to advance the mission for freedom in America and beyond.

Such a time as this we called upon again to defend our freedom for our children & generations to come!

7. THE HOUR!

My hope and prayer is that America as a Nation & We as a People will Change the direction of our thinking for our Children and generations to come.

What is that change? Can we do it?

"If We Are Not Working In The Best Interests Of Our Family, Who's Interests Are We Working Fore?"

That is the question of the hour for all of us to answer! Our children and families depend on it.

Their welfare and support are tied to it from that was fought and died fore. Can we do no less than to affirm that a Country as big as the United States with all of its vast resources is a

34

country big enough to support its children and generations to come?

Can we no less bring attention to the fact that America is only as great as her children and families?
We must consider the consequences of our social behavior that fails to recognize the value and worth of a solid family structure. It is this premise that our culture and society rests.

Certainly, the current history of American culture dictates to all of us to take inventory of ourselves and our culture and its impact on our children and their Best Interests.

Nothing can replace for a child loving parents who work to see that they have value and worth and know they are loved. The economic and social impact that results in creating strong families is immeasurable and

35

necessary to maintain and sustain stable communities not only in America but throughout the World. My hope is that the message of *The Promise* will motivate all of us to do, act and speak the *values* and *principles* that were fought and died to preserve, protect and defend *Freedom & Liberty* for our children and generations to come.

Let us dedicate ourselves to speaking the facts to make our reality a living experience to form a more perfect Union for all of us now and forevermore.

Our success is producing *No Child Left Behind.*

That means we dedicate ourselves to their success and communicate that in our culture and our World.

Anything less would be *Uncivilized!*

36

<u>**NOTES**</u>

8. THE NOW!

"Fore If You Are Not Working In The Best

Interests Of Your Family, Then Whose Interests Are You Working Fore?" – said the Wise Man.

What I have said and truly believe *is* that this Generation of Americans and Citizens of the World have an unprecedented opportunity to change the course of *History* for the benefit of our children and generations to come.

As I repeated in my first book, AMERICA 2000:

"Foundations For Generations!", my belief that this time in *History* is predicated on the belief that we are living in a time capsule or

38

coming of Age to the realities of our time and that both Words & Family matter to the *preservation and protection* of society now and generations to come!

My hope is that America as a nation and We as a People will find it in our hearts to adopt for our Children a Code of Conduct conducive to producing a consistent result in the lives and attitudes for the benefit of our children and generations to come so much so that we abandon the negative selfish behavior for the good decent and honest one.

There is absolutely no reason for any child to be left behind in the World including the United States.

It is up to us to hold those accountable who *use, abuse and misuse* us or anyone for

39

personal gain at the expense of our family and children.

Blaming others is not the solution. Motivating Ourselves and others *Is!* A Nation of Laws requires an *Activist Society.* Not destructive but *Productive!*

The ability to make decisions based on fact not Fiction where problems become stepping stones for Long term opportunity. This is the vision our Nation must adopt with policies and procedures that work in THE BEST INTERSTS of the family.

That is "THE BALL DOCTRINE" Creating Peace & Prosperity In Every Nation! for every child and every parent in every generation!

In my other books, I speak of Service to Others I share with President Kennedy's vision of the Peace Corp. Ameria Corp. Votechnical training and Schools that prepare our young people in *Skill Sets.*

No Child left behind *means banishing illiteracy educating the masses* and putting value of worth back into the culture. The results are astounding and the future bright for our children & generations to come.

"*As* a result, No Child Left Behind!"

The Patriots believed that the value of life was predicated on the belief in oneself and one's ability to survive and thrive. This was born out by their determination to beat the odds to survive and thrive.

41

Is that not the same challenge that all of us have Born into life itself? Are we not all put the tests of others to survive and thrive?

What we are witnessing is a clash of civilizations colliding since the end of World War II that cause concern regarding the established value systems supported by generations of Americans and those in the New World of Enlightenment.

Our history as a people and we as a nation of Immigrants gives us a unique opportunity to change the course of history for ourselves, our children and our posterity by conforming to established beliefs and attitudes that support the *"family"* to keep to strong again!

How are we going to do it? As I have written in several paragraphs of this and other

42

treatments of my work, Central to the arguments of the family is the matter of *"sustainability"* from within its core.

The relationships and the communication is key for the survival to full maturity by its members especially those of the children or parents without partners. Society pays a "heavy price" when those within it become the *"enemy"* within.

Just like during the time of the revolution, some of us were sucked into a battle initially we could not win but feared we could not lose. Is this not the same challenge we face to today? Are we so dumb to think we could never be challenged to stand united to fight the forces of despotism and tyranny again but this time on our own shores as it was then?

Because economics is such an intrinsic part of our culture, we are forced to face the facts that a weak economy makes for a harder life experience.

But what makes it better is when we all pull together for the betterment of our Children and Generations to come.

Like soldiers of old marching off to war, the Battles we face are internal and self-driven by a generation of privilege that mirrors the same attitudes that governments demonstrated at the height of conflicts from the American Revolution to the American Civil War which for more than 150 years later which has brought us to where we are, NOW!

My fervent prayer for all of us is that we will decide to correct our problems with the knowledge that will *insure* the future for our children by doing what is necessary with facts that make a difference to preserve, protect and defend the integrity of the family structure and make it possible for it not only

to survive but thrive under the Constitution of the United States of America.

What that means is "*Creating The Means To Support The Ends For An ACCOUNTABLE*

Society", starting at the top working our way down to the bottom. I speak of "*sustainability*" lifting the middle class from the bottom up by the code word, BALLONOMICS! What does that mean?

Like in a match of chess, the players

position themselves to checkmate; meaning they employ all the tools of strategy to assist them in making a winning play. It is no different in life for that which one can control to bring about the desired result.

However, that creates a problem for those who decide to play by their own rules to the detriment of the family structure.

For Court sponsored corruption, time is on the side of those who discover and live in it. For us who have been damaged by it, the tyranny of the State and their abuse so near, means we are placed in a position to challenge and correct it.

GREED corrupts *"entirely"* those in a Position of Power and Duty to refrain from its temptation.

46

How can we be sure that we don't become a victim ourselves or the perpetrator of that which brings devastation to those we care?

As I have communicated, the 'Best Interests of Family' is the real issue society must address for it to find its way back to normalcy and legitimacy in an open society; fore those that are not, the future for them is to create an environment of change they decide will support and sustain their families in a democratic process, otherwise violent CHANGE may come as it did in 1776 & 1860.

9. THE FIRE!

What is wrong to call out Society when it exercises power and control over its citizens to the detriment of the family in America? What is wrong when it works against its Best Interests? What is wrong for us to decide the system is broken and must change to support its children & their parents?

The answer is, ***Nothing***!

"Fore I am convinced that the same energy and motivation that sustained the *Patriots* of old still burns brightly amongst some of us today."

How do we know?

The Spirit Of America was born out of struggle, A testament to the men and women

48

who gave their full measure so that this nation could remain free from threats both foreign and domestic.

For that we are a grateful nation, conceived in *Liberty* for the masses and the ruling classes. A Nation of Laws created by the legislature of each State to manage and regulate interstate commerce for the wellbeing of our Citizens and our family.

The *Federalist papers* spoke to that whereby that which is the United States Constitution is moot can be read from those who took the time to examine the issues that impact our lives with others *still* waiting to be resolved upon WE the governed.

American Exceptionalism was born also and continues to this day making history for

49

a more perfect Union that Abraham Lincoln referred to in his Gettysburg Address.

What that means to us creates within us a desire to intervene into the affairs of Nations that causes us as a People to take inventory of the conduct of Nations detrimental to the wellbeing of America and her people. Ultimately, it causes us to support or deny our support to rogue nations & dictatorships that work against the Public & National interests of the United States, her people, families and allies.

This then, in a broad stroke of the pen can be described as the struggle for power and control that continues even today to place *America* in the cross-hairs of *history.* How We The People at this time in history will define for generations to come, events that will show *Exceptional leadership* because of doctrine of THE BEST INTERESTS of all family especially those involving children.

I am reminded by generations past the tasks they surmounted to build this nation to keep it free for their children and generations to come. That is a recurring theme within theses United States by We The People have an ongoing responsibility to fulfill.

The Story in the Fall of 1781 would not be complete if it were not for the French government participating in the establishment for victory at Yorktown, Virginia that crowded *Autumn Day, October 19, 1781.*

"MY Lord, I Beseech Thee, You Must Order The Surrender!"

British General Charles O'Hara

Appealing to

British General Charles Cornwallis

BATTLE OF YORKTOWN, VA 10/19/1781

*Earlier……*Why should I trade One tyrant 3000 miles away for 3000 tyrants One mile away?"

'An elected Legislature can trample a man's Rights as easily as a King.' *

*Benjamin Martin, The Patriot, Sony Pictures 2000.

Is this not the condition we find ourselves fighting today within our own country? Are we not the heirs of that which was paid fore in blood?

Does that not resonate with We, The American People? Have we become so arrogant as to believe we are entitled to a life of ME,ME,ME,ME & ME!?, while the rest of us suffer from the actions of others? Like *Patrick Henry* iterated, *"God Forbid It Not!"* * "With the War ending and our Militia disbanding, I take measure in what we have lost and what we have won." *–Benjamin Martin, The Patriot*

*Patrick Henry, March 23, 1775 Falls Church, Virginia.

What We The People have lost and We The People have won: The SOCIAL CONTRACT of 1781. Like Lincoln, our history continues to be perfected by the struggles mankind engages both in America and beyond. Our great hope is that WE THE PEOPLE will recognize abuse when it comes and be motivated to do what is necessary to defeat it. This then again, is *The Promise* we all inherit.

THE BEST INTERSTS OF THE FAMILY

demands of us to do no less to insure domestic tranquility for our children and generations to come. Why? Because if you are not working in their Best Interests, whose interests are you working fore?

This is THE PROMISE! Working in the

Best Interests of your family! Life is about the Best Interests of family by *speaking it into BEING!*

The 5th Commandment:

"Honor Thy Father and Thy Mother So That You May Live a Long and Good Life!" NIV GOD puts a premium on family that he created for the preservation and protection of society and because He is a Spirit, He sees everything all the time. The Apostle Paul spoke to the Greeks, "For In Him We Live, Move & Have Our Being."Acts 17:28

GOD gives us *choices* and we are all accountable to them and to Him. By understanding this premise, our decisions move in the direction He intends for our Best Interests and our future! All we need do is make the right ones!

SELF GOVERNANCE is the hardest thing in Life for Society to comprehend and find the muster to do. IT taxes our time, family and our resources.

It puts us on notice We The People are responsible for the actions of our neighbors because they too came from a family, good or bad. The fact we exist is testimony that a higher power governs the Universe and we with it. The Promise corresponds.

It is our legacy to preserve, protect and defend our culture for the preservation of our *Nation* for our children to make America a better place for them and in their Best Interests! Should we ask any less of ourselves for that which has been given? I rest that question with you.

It means CITIZEN CANDIDATES; not professional politicians take responsibility to insure that the "traditional family" is well represented in The Halls of Congress and the by ways of Local & State government.

Union shops that impose unrealistic burdensome expectations upon labor and management driving up the cost of production making their product non-competitive in a global marketplace. This must change. Bring back & keep MADE IN AMERICA, for our children and generations to come.

10. THE FINISH!

"With The War Ending and Our Militia Disbanding,

I Take Measure In What We Have Lost & Won"

Benjamin Martin – The Patriot.

The reasons for the American Revolution of 1776 against the British Crown of England resulted in the greatest transfer of wealth in the Western Hemisphere. One could say that the Discovery of Americas began the process of Globalization which continues even now.

This transfer made possible the opportunity for a nation of immigrants to realize their potential under the Color Of Law. What made them special was their motivation to connect with the land and make it their own. Land ownership was the driving force behind the War for Independence. It remains today.

Cheap labor fueled the conquest to create wealth from the sweat of slaves who were imported to do tasks waiting on Southern plantations with coal and gold mines for exploitation.

With Cheap labor, State governments could tax the land and fund their enterprise. Government in the local community could too making for more control and regulation for any business to comply to their demands. This power & control monopoly over the Citizenry contributed greatly to the demise of American free enterprise making it more difficult to succeed for parents and their children. I believe this contributed greatly to the welfare state to buy votes after the emancipation act and ratification of the thirteenth amendment to the Constitution. For these and other reasons the need to *reset* has come.

"Creating the means to support the ends" has always been the driving force of entrepreneurship and the guiding principle behind "free enterprise capitalism".

Your money, property, liquidity stays in your pocket; not government. Big government is big trouble for all of us. It demands we comply to them.

That problem created the wars that created the death depleting families of their loved ones by destroying their family legacies probating out their estates prior to death incarcerating loved ones in nursing homes separating themselves from their money & property.

Immoral, unethical & unlawful behavior by the Courts; the taking advantage of families by those Government agencies whose sole purpose is to exploit your assets to the State.

The *stealing* of family members either by abuse of power by law enforcement agencies, police using tactical maneuvers to arrest and incarcerate in support of government agencies making money by Federal programs both against our youth & seniors.

"IT IS OUTRAGEOUS & MUST STOP!"

2ND Amendment Rights were put into the Bill Of Rights to support 1st Amendment Rights and the Right of Free Association amongst family members.

These rights are being violated everyday to cage us into compliance with government dictum. Officials love to control us for their own purposes. Those purposes are not in our Best Interests nor that of your family. Wake up! Your Country is on fire!

Our World is changing and we must change to make it accountable and better for all the people who cannot and will not be bought off by empty promises from *those* that work against the Best Interests of the family everywhere but working for their own interests anywhere.

"Fore If You Are Not Working In The

BEST INTERESTS Of Your Family, Whose Interests Are You Working Fore?" – author unknown

I am constantly reminded for whom I am Working fore. The Children of America and Generations to come! These are the generations of children that must have a chance to survive and thrive in a global economy starting with the key principle of entrepreneurship:

"Creating The Means To Support The Ends!"

Not the ends justifying the means!

Globalism is a failed policy throughout Europe; United States Shipping off American Industry to foreign countries is a failed policy

63

that has wrecked America's economy & institutions because of a bloated government bureaucracy tax system working against all families.

Every nation has the right to produce products and services for its own children and families.

Every nation has the right to banish illiteracy replaced with skilled labor. Every nation has the right to maintain its own culture in the Best Interests of its own children and families. These Are some of the Rights every Nation is entitled.

If these are some of the Rights Of Nations, *What Other Rights Should They Possess?*

The Right of passage to be free from the

dictum Of Power & Control by political parties stacking the Deck against workers and their families. Such abuse manifests itself within the social fabric turning good people and their children into criminals by being taken advantage both financially and personally.

Children being held captive against parents whose only crime was some concocted allegation of abuse separating loved ones by the State so that they could balance their budgets on the backs of our kids. Deplorable Unredeemable! Our Bill of Rights & Constitution were created to protect our populations from government abuse. Sadly, the abuse continues without any accountability by our elected or appointed officials. What can we do?

"Let Justice Be Done Though The Heavens Fall!"

Justice for whom?, for what? The moral and ethical equivalents that cause peace or war? Our history would be incomplete if we failed to examine these questions to empower us to correct and understand the duty that exists to make things right for our children and generations to come.

A pervasive theme that continues to damage all of us is the view that cultural and legal problems are deplorable and uncorrectable. That is a false premise by those who created the problem.

Problems created within an existing system require a new model to replace the old with the new. A new model will consider the

66

nature and scope of the problem and rally others to assist in correcting them. Much of this is created by unaccountable behavior coming from business, labor and government waging war upon the Best Interests of the traditional "family".

"Problems Created Within An Existing System Requires A New Model To Replace The Old With The New." Not A New Constitution Restoration Attitudes Toward That Constitution and Free Enterprise Capitalism: The Magic of a Free Nation Devoid of Power & Control Strategy.

Why? Because it works against the family's ability to survive and thrive. Corporatism does nothing to secure the future of a nation nor her children. Big government creates the same as does labor unions. Power

& control is the game.

The result is the same. No one gets rich by feeding A pig that consumes more than it produces.

Because government makes nothing, its job is to protect The People in the course of *public safety*.

How it manages to do so becomes a subject also for Americans to consider and question, especially given Global Terrorism.

I cannot underestimate the resolve some nations demonstrate to *defeat* classical democracy by the Common Good of The People it fails to affirm.

Unfortunately, our leaders seldom speak of

the root problem causing these conflicts and tensions which by nature are inherently connected with traditional "family" attitudes of it's Best Interests & decisions that benefit rather than damage persistent to *steal* it's assets, property & emotional wellbeing.

Americans are being tested as to whether this Nation or any nation has the capacity to Stand and Defeat the forces of nature that would jeopardize their future *success* based on democratic processes.

Inherent in all of this is the Traditional Family and how Society wishes to treat her will be the outcome for all of us; that is a promise.

Let us agree and resolve within ourselves that America as a Nation and We as a People will Stop and Listen to Sound Doctrine that appeals to our sense of value and worth. Many sacrifices were made for us by others leading to their deaths and full measure. Can we do any less to insure for those we love including our children and more?

Are we to become a Nation of Narcissists or Nation Proud in her heritage and her principles?

Can we learn from others and decide to *correct* the mistakes of our collective past?

Are we Worthy to continue the traditions for those who gave their all that we might have a burst of freedom and the support to pursue personal happiness without taking advantage of others, their property and their money? That is the question.

Greed is a terrible disease and with it comes death, to a person and to a nation. Families determine both. A nation of laws does too, especially if they are not enforced by Courts that allow them to damage and destroy innocent citizens out of their money, property and their family.

Fore this was the concern at the beginning of the Republic for that which was remembered and learned from the history of Europe and the impact *The Promise* created within the *Social Contract.*

www.ingramcontent.com/pod-product-compliance
Lightning Source LLC
Chambersburg PA
CBHW062111280526
45788CB00003B/1431